THE ENCYCLOPEDIA LUMBERJANICA

An Illustrated Guide to the
Hardcore Lady-Types
of Lumberjanes

Published by
BOOM! BOX

P9-DGB-151

Ross Richie CEO & Founder
Joy Huffman CFO
Matt Gagnon Editor-in-Chief
Filip Sablik President, Publishing & Marketing
Stephen Christy President, Development
Lance Kreiter Vice President, Licensing & Merchandising
Arune Singh Vice President, Marketing
Bryce Carlson Vice President, Editorial & Creative Strategy
Kate Henning Director, Operations
Spencer Simpson Director, Sales
Scott Newman Manager, Production Design
Elyse Strandberg Manager, Finance
Sierra Hahn Executive Editor
Jeanine Schaefer Executive Editor
Dafna Pleban Senior Editor
Shannon Watters Senior Editor
Eric Harburn Senior Editor
Matthew Levine Editor
Sophie Philips-Roberts Associate Editor
Amanda LaFranco Associate Editor
Jonathan Manning Associate Editor
Gavin Gronenthal Assistant Editor
Gwen Waller Assistant Editor
Allyson Gronowitz Assistant Editor
Ramiro Portnoy Assistant Editor
Kenzie Rzonca Assistant Editor
Shelby Netschke Editorial Assistant
Michelle Ankley Design Coordinator
Marie Krupina Production Designer
Grace Park Production Designer
Chelsea Roberts Production Designer
Samantha Knapp Production Design Assistant
José Meza Live Events Lead
Stephanie Hocutt Digital Marketing Lead
Esther Kim Marketing Coordinator
Breanna Sarpy Live Events Coordinator
Amanda Lawson Marketing Assistant
Holly Aitchison Digital Sales Coordinator
Morgan Perry Retail Sales Coordinator
Megan Christopher Operations Coordinator
Rodrigo Hernandez Operations Coordinator
Zipporah Smith Operations Assistant
Jason Lee Senior Accountant
Sabrina Lesin Accounting Assistant

Designer **MARIE KRUPINA**

Assistant Editor **KENZIE RZONCA**

Editor **SOPHIE PHILIPS-ROBERTS**

Executive Editor **JEANINE SCHAEFER**

BOOM! BOX ENCYCLOPEDIA LUMBERJANICA: AN ILLUSTRATED GUIDE TO THE HARDCORE LADY-TYPES OF LUMBERJANES, September 2020. Published by BOOM! Box, a division of Boom Entertainment, Inc. Lumberjanes is ™ & © 2020 Shannon Watters, Grace Ellis, Noelle Stevenson & Brooklyn Allen. All rights reserved. BOOM! Box™ and the BOOM! Box logo are trademarks of Boom Entertainment, Inc., registered in various countries and categories. All characters, events, and institutions depicted herein are fictional. Any similarity between any of the names, characters, persons, events, and/or institutions in this publication to actual names, characters, and persons, whether living or dead, events, and/or institutions is unintended and purely coincidental. BOOM! Box does not read or accept unsolicited submissions of ideas, stories, or artwork.

BOOM! Studios, 5670 Wilshire Boulevard, Suite 400, Los Angeles, CA 90036-5679.
Printed in China. First Printing.

ISBN: 978-1-68415-599-6, eISBN: 978-1-64668-011-5

THE ENCYCLOPEDIA
LUMBERJANICA ™

Written by
SUSAN COINER-COLLIER

Illustrated by
KANESHA C. BRYANT
KAITI INFANTE
ALEXIA KHODANIAN
JULIA MADRIGAL

Cover by
KAT LEYH & CHELSEA ROBERTS

Spot Illustrations by
BROOKLYN ALLEN
DOZERDRAWS
KAT LEYH
AYME SOTUYO

*Special thanks to **Kelsey Pate** for giving the Lumberjanes their name.*

Created by
SHANNON WATTERS, GRACE ELLIS,
NOELLE STEVENSON & BROOKLYN ALLEN

THE LUMBERJANES PLEDGE

I solemnly swear to do my best
Every day, and in all that I do,
To be brave and strong,
To be truthful and compassionate,
To be interesting and interested,
To pay attention and question
The world around me,
To think of others first,
To always help and protect my friends,
~~To respect the programs and faith in God,~~

THEN THERE'S A
LINE ABOUT GOD,
OR WHATEVER

And to make the world a better place
For Lumberjane scouts
And for everyone else.

INTRODUCTION

Not all of a Lumberjane's training takes place in the great outdoors! A modern Lumberjane knows that many girls and women came before her to clear the paths she now treads. From women like lady pirate Ching Shih of the 19th century Qing dynasty, to the modern transgender rights activist and politician Sarah McBride, history is filled with interesting, passionate, curious women who seized the bull by the horns and left their mark on the world. While not all of these women were Lumberjanes (in fact, sadly, none of them were), they still serve as admirable role models for all Lumberjane scouts. Girls would do well to study these trailblazers and learn from their trials, tribulations, and triumphs. A Lumberjane must know the past in order to prepare for the future!

JULIETTE GORDON LOW

Juliette Gordon Low is an important figure for all Lumberjanes to know, because she founded the Girl Scouts of the United States in 1912. More than a hundred years later, girls are still making friends and having adventures with the organization she started in her hometown of Savannah, Georgia. Born Juliette Gordon in 1860, immediately before the American Civil War, she led a comfortable but not particularly noteworthy life, until a chance meeting with the founder of the Boy Scouts changed her path.

Low was known as Daisy to friends and family throughout her life. A funny, fun-loving, somewhat eccentric person (her family called her "Crazy Daisy"), she was prone to doing things like going fishing in an evening gown, or, on one noteworthy occasion, standing on her head during a Girl Scouts board meeting to show off the newly-designed Girl Scout shoes she was wearing. Creative and lively, she struggled with spelling (it's thought that she might have been dyslexic), and loved art, animals, and the outdoors.

Although her early childhood was marked by the upheaval of post-Civil War Reconstruction, Daisy's family recovered well, and she had a privileged and happy childhood. After an education at a series of boarding schools, she studied art in New York and traveled to Europe. In those days, the primary goal in life of a woman of Daisy's social class was marriage to a suitable man, and Daisy spent her early 20s in a whirlwind of social activities designed to introduce her to appropriate suitors. Daisy also frequently dealt with bouts of malaria and ear infections, which eventually led to a ruptured eardrum when Daisy was 24. Her ears gave her trouble for the rest of her life. At times she could hear quite well, but at other times she was more severely deafened.

When Daisy was 19, her younger sister Alice died of scarlet fever. During the period of mourning that followed, Daisy met William Mackay Low, known as Willy, who would later become her husband. Unfortunately, Daisy and Willy's marriage proved to be unhappy, as sometimes happens when two people aren't suited for each other, and Willy died when Daisy was forty-five.

So, Daisy took some time to adjust to the new circumstances of her life. She purchased a house in London and settled there near her younger sister, Mabel, who was married with two children. She kept up a busy social life and traveled extensively, dabbling in a few charitable ventures. She felt driven to contribute positively to the world in some way, but wasn't sure how.

In 1911, she met Robert Baden-Powell, the founder of the Boy Scouts, when she was seated beside him at a dinner party. This chance meeting transformed her life. She and Baden-Powell immediately formed a close friendship; he even proposed marriage to her, although she turned him down. She became involved in the Girl Guides organization, the counterpart to the Boy Scouts, leading a patrol group near

her summer home in Scotland, and that winter organizing two additional groups in London. The Girl Guides were the exact opportunity Daisy had been waiting for, and she threw herself wholeheartedly into the endeavor.

In early 1912, she and Baden-Powell travelled to the United States by steamer ship for Daisy to return home and for Baden-Powell to tour the country in support of the Boy Scouts. Immediately upon her arrival in Savannah, Daisy established the first patrol of Girl Guides in the United States and set about making the fun and learning of the Girl Guides available to girls across the country.

The early years of the American Girl Guides were occupied with expansion and jockeying for position with competitors. With the popularity of the Boy Scouts, many similar organizations for girls arose, and all wanted to be considered the official counterpart of the Boy Scouts. Daisy tirelessly campaigned for her Girl Guides, and the organization expanded rapidly, even though Daisy continued to spend much of her time in England. She found competent people to help her, and soon the organization changed its name to the Girl Scouts, opened a national headquarters in Washington, DC, and grew its membership into the thousands.

With the entry of the United States into World War I, the Girl Scouts gained national recognition and acclaim for their assistance with the war effort. They made bandages, knitted socks for soldiers, planted kitchen gardens, sold Liberty bonds...and some in the United Kingdom even acted as spies! The organization thrived. After Daisy voluntarily stepped down as president in 1920, she devoted the rest of her life to expanding the Girl Scouts internationally.

By the time of her death at age 66 from breast cancer, the Girl Scouts were established in countries from China to Latvia. Daisy died at home in Savannah, surrounded by her family, with the legacy of the Girl Scouts secure.

It's undeniable that Daisy's financial circumstances and social connections were critical to the success of the Girl Scouts—she bankrolled the organization and paid everyone's salaries for the first several years. She had little experience with management or formal philanthropy, and her family initially treated the Girl Scouts as a passing fancy, which they expected her to abandon before long. However, Daisy remained committed, and it seems that her fun-loving, somewhat out-of-the-box personality allowed her to succeed. She had a talent for picking smart, capable people to work with, and her passion, drive, and irrepressible enthusiasm were key in the Girl Scouts' success. Thanks to Daisy Low's vision, girls all over the world are still enjoying the many benefits of scouting.

100 YEARS OF GIRL SCOUT UNIFORMS.

- The original Girl Scouts uniform was based on that of the British Girl Guides: a dark blue skirt and matching blouse with a light blue tie around the neck, black stockings, shoes, and a wide-brimmed hat.

- By 1914, Daisy decided to switch the fabric to khaki to match the uniform of the American Boy Scouts.

- By the 1950s, uniforms were green and had introduced the iconic sash.

- Modern Girl Scouts have more flexibility with what they wear.

OCTAVIA E. BUTLER

A prolific and acclaimed writer of novels and short stories, Octavia E. Butler won the Hugo and Nebula awards for her fiction. She was the first writer of science fiction and fantasy to receive the MacArthur Fellowship, colloquially known as the "Genius Grant," and for a time, she was the most prominent Black woman writing science fiction. Her ground-breaking work provided incisive commentary on race, gender, and sexuality while thrillingly exploring new ideas and new worlds.

Octavia was born in Pasadena, California in 1947. Her father died when she was a toddler, and she was raised by her mother and grandmother. Her mother worked as a maid, and Octavia later talked about spending her childhood feeling ashamed of the work her mother did.

She said she didn't like seeing her mother going through back doors and being talked about like she was invisible.

Octavia's interest in writing began in childhood. She was a shy child, and described herself as socially awkward. An avid reader, she discovered science fiction magazines as she worked her way through the children's section of the local library. While her own stories were initially about horses, at the age of twelve she happened to watch a "terrible" science fiction movie on TV (*Devil Girl from Mars*) and decided she could do better. She produced her first science fiction story not long after, and the year after that, began submitting stories to magazines.

She attended Pasadena City College for an associate's degree, where she took several writing classes and won a short story contest. She later studied at California State University, Los Angeles, although she never finished a degree there. In 1969, in her early twenties, Butler began taking classes at the Screen Writers' Guild through their Open Door Program.

She had no interest in screenwriting, but the classes were free. The program was designed to mentor minority writers—as Octavia put it, "They looked around and said to each other, 'Why are we all white?'". In her second semester, she took a class with the science fiction writer Harlan Ellison. He encouraged her to apply for the Clarion Science Fiction Writers' Workshop in Pennsylvania. During the six weeks of the workshop, she sold her first two stories, an early success, which was followed by a drought of five years during which she sold nothing at all.

In the meantime, Octavia held down a series of blue-collar jobs that required her to get up very early in the morning (at 2 or 3 AM) to write. Although her mother hoped Octavia would find reliable work as a secretary, she was supportive of Octavia's ambitions as a writer, or at least tolerant of them; she gave Octavia the money she needed to attend Clarion. In late 1974, Octavia began to write her first novel, *Patternmaster*, which was published in 1976.

Two sequels followed soon after, and then *Kindred*, which was published as mainstream fiction instead of science fiction. Perhaps Octavia's most famous work, *Kindred* tells the story of a modern-day woman time-traveling back to the time of slavery. Rooted in slave narratives, *Kindred* unflinchingly presents its subject matter, although Octavia emphasized that she sanitized the truth because she thought there were limits to what readers would be willing to tolerate. After finishing the *Patternist* series, her next works, the *Xenogenesis* trilogy, were more straightforward science fiction. By the time of their publications, Octavia was making a living from her writing and speaking engagements, and was able to travel to Peru to do research for the series.

In the early 1990s, Octavia dealt with a period of writer's block that lasted several years. She finally broke through with *The Parable of the Sower* in 1993, and in 1995 was awarded the MacArthur Fellowship.

A few years later, after her mother died, she moved from Southern California to Lake Forest Park, Washington, just north of Seattle. She first visited the city in the 1970s and had always wanted to live there.

A self-described hermit, Octavia lived with a large collection of books and audio tapes. She was somewhat dyslexic and preferred to listen to books on tape rather than read. She loved National Public Radio and would often tape record broadcasts to listen to on the bus or as she walked, as she didn't drive. She was a curious and widely read person, and everything she read informed her writing. She more than once cited the novel *Dune*, by Frank Herbert, as her favorite work of science fiction, but often resisted naming specific authors as influences on her own writing—she liked to say that she read everything, both good and bad.

Octavia died in 2006 after a fall near her home. She left behind a rich legacy of work that continues to enlighten and inspire.

OCTAVIA BUTLER'S GUIDELINES FOR WRITING.

- Write every day, no excuses.

- Read every day, voraciously and omnivorously.

- Take classes or workshops to get feedback from others.

- Revise your work. If you think, "This doesn't matter. It's good enough," go back and fix the flaw.

- Persist!

SARAH ROBLES

Sarah Robles is a weightlifter and Olympian who won a bronze medal at the 2016 Olympic Games in Rio de Janeiro, becoming the first American to medal in weightlifting at the Olympics since 2000 (the very first year women were able to compete in weightlifting at the Olympics). Sarah competes in the super heavyweight division, an awesome reminder that bodies of all shapes and sizes can be strong and healthy. Her commitment to her sport despite the challenges she's dealt with throughout her life—a lack of financial support and the death of her father—is an inspiration to all girls who pursue a dream.

Sarah was born in 1988 in San Diego, California, and grew up in Desert Hot Springs, just north of Palm Springs and nearby San Jacinto. She has one older brother. She was self-conscious about her body as a child, but when she began to participate in track and field sports in middle school, she realized that her height and size could be an advantage.

In high school, she was a top-ranked shot-putter and discus thrower, and she eventually won scholarships to the University of Alabama and later Arizona State University. She also began weightlifting in high school, as part of her training, and took part in some local competitions. Her father died the same year that she graduated from high school, which presented a difficult emotional challenge.

In 2008, while at Arizona State, she took up weightlifting again. After only a few months, she qualified for the National Junior Championships, where she came in third in her weight class. She made the team for the World Junior Championships and placed second, at which point she forfeited her shot-put scholarship to commit full-time to weightlifting.

At the 2011 World Championships, Sarah finished 11th in her weight class, but with a performance strong enough to make her the top-ranked American weightlifter out of all the competitors. Not long after that, she qualified for the 2012 Olympics as one of two American women in her weight class. Sarah didn't expect to medal in London—the world record was above her personal best by about 150 pounds—but she was thrilled to have the chance to compete. Despite her athletic prowess, Sarah struggled financially while training for the Games. Her training schedule didn't permit outside paid work, and leading up to the London Olympics, she lived on a $400-a-month stipend from USA Weightlifting. That money was barely enough to feed her. She relied on food banks and donations from friends and family, and her coach at the time trained her for free. While many Olympians rely on sponsorships and endorsements for income, weightlifting isn't a popular sport in the United States, and Sarah wasn't well-known enough to land any big deals. She has also spoken out about biases toward smaller athletes in more typically-feminine sports.

Sarah persevered despite these financial problems, which might have prompted a different athlete to hang up their weightlifting shoes for good. In London, she placed 7th and achieved a number of personal best lifts (known as PRs, for Personal Records). She considered quitting weightlifting after London, but after a heart-to-heart with her coach, she decided to keep training.

Unfortunately, in 2013, Sarah received a two-year sanction (meaning she couldn't compete for two years) after she tested positive for DHEA (dehydroepiandrosterone—that's a mouthful!), a steroid hormone, at the Pan American Games. In her official statement on the matter, Sarah revealed that her doctor had recommended DHEA supplementation to help with her polycystic ovarian syndrome (PCOS), a common hormonal disorder. However, Sarah had not filed for approval prior to her drug test, and her appeal of the suspension was denied. She was banned from the sport for two years.

But Sarah didn't quit. She found a new coach and moved to Houston, Texas, where she worked and trained. When the time came to begin competing again, she was ready. She immediately began participating in meets, including World Championships, where she placed 6th. She qualified for the Rio de Janeiro Olympics at the US Olympic Trials in May 2016 and immediately began gearing up for her next Olympics. In Rio de Janeiro, she set a new personal best and medaled, taking bronze in her weight class.

Since her triumph at the 2016 Olympics, Sarah has continued to train and compete. In 2018, she broke an American record for the clean and jerk which had stood for 13 years. She won the gold medal for her weight class at the 2019 Pan American Games in Lima, Peru. The next Olympics in Tokyo aren't far off! Keep an eye on Sarah as she aims to keep improving, setting new records, and winning medals.

THE TWO OLYMPICS LIFTS (CLEAN & JERK AND SNATCH).

There are two lifts in Olympic weightlifting: the clean and jerk, and the snatch.

- In the clean and jerk, the lifter powerfully moves ("cleans") the bar from the floor to a position across his or her shoulders, then "jerks" the bar above the head with the arms extended.

- For the snatch, the bar is lifted from the ground to overhead in one motion, after which the lifter stands from a deep squat.

NAKANO TAKEKO

Nakano Takeko, a female samurai warrior, famously fought during the Boshin War of 1868-1869 that ended the Tokugawa shogunate, Japan's last feudal military government. In the years since her death in battle, Takeko (Japanese names are presented with the family name first) has become something of a folk hero. A monument to her still stands at a temple in the town of Aizubange, and during the autumn festival, girls take part in a procession to honor her memory.

Takeko belonged to a long tradition of female martial artists and warriors. Even before the rise of the samurai in the 12th century, some women trained in the use of weapons to defend their homes and families during times of war. We know from archaeological excavations that women were present on Japanese battlefields. A number of colorful woman warriors dot Japanese history, and while historians sometimes question whether they were real people, they remain popular figures in folklore and fiction.

As early as the year 200 CE, the Empress Jingu is said to have led an invasion of Korea—while pregnant with the future emperor, no less. The warrior Tomoe Gozen features in the famous epic *The Tale of the Heike*. ("Gozen" is not a name but a term of address that can be translated as "lady.") It's important to understand that Takeko wasn't an aberration, but instead fit into an established and accepted role for women.

Born in Edo (now Tokyo) in 1847, Takeko was the oldest of three children of an official from Aizu, in what's now Fukushima Prefecture in northeast Japan. Not much is known about her early life. She began training in martial arts at a young age and became particularly skilled with the naginata, a long pole weapon with a blade on one end. The naginata was considered a good weapon for women, since its length allowed the user to keep an opponent at a distance, minimizing any differences in body size and upper body strength.

In the mid-1800s, Japan was grappling with the choice of remaining closed off and isolated, or opening to further contact with Western nations. The Tokugawa shogunate had kept access to the country limited for over two hundred years. After the country was forcibly opened to American trade in

1852, a period of upheaval ensued and different political factions sought power.

Conflict between the two main factions, the shogunate and the supporters of the young emperor, reached a peak during the Boshin War. Aizu, like other northern domains, was loyal to the shogun and resisted the imperialists. When the imperial army set about defeating the northern domains, Aizu-Wakamatsu Castle became the site of a month-long siege in October and November of 1868.

The women of Aizu received extensive combat training and were prepared to fight alongside their male family

members. Twenty or thirty formed a highly-trained unit fighting on the front lines. Takeko was one of them; her mother and younger sister were two others.

These women played a key role in a battle a few days into the siege. Wielding naginata and swords, Takeko and her fellow women warriors charged imperial troops who were armed with rifles. When they realized they were facing women, the imperial soldiers held their fire in hopes of taking the women alive, but this exposed them to attack. The women were determined not to be taken prisoner and attacked ferociously. Takeko killed five or six men before receiving a fatal bullet wound at the peak of the battle.

After her death, Takeko was taken to a nearby temple for cremation. Her tombstone still stands at this same temple, and her naginata is preserved there.

The castle's defenders were eventually forced to surrender to the imperial troops, and the Boshin War concluded with a solidification of the emperor's power. The modernization of Japan had begun.

BELL HOOKS

Writer, teacher, activist, and scholar, bell hooks has published more than 30 books and has profoundly influenced academic and mainstream discourse on race and gender. Since the publication of her first major book in 1981, she has established herself as an important thinker and critic. In addition to her scholarly work, she's published widely in mainstream publications and has written books for children, including the popular *Happy to Be Nappy*. Through her lectures and participation on panels, she's become known outside of academic circles and is considered one of the most important public intellectuals of her generation.

The name bell hooks is a pseudonym, taken in honor of her great-grandmother, "a woman who spoke her mind." She chose not to capitalize her pen name to emphasize her ideas instead of herself as a person. bell was born Gloria Jean Watkins in Hopkinsville, Kentucky in 1952, one of seven siblings: six girls and a boy. Her mother worked as a homemaker and sometimes as a maid, and her father was a janitor.

Growing up as a Black girl, bell was sharply conscious of differences in gender and race from early in her childhood. Hopkinsville was segregated, and bell has written of watching white children being bused in to their schools and wondering why she wasn't allowed to ride the buses. Likewise, she and her only brother were very close in age, and as they were playmates and constant companions, she saw the differences

in how they were treated and in their expected roles. These early experiences formed the basis for her life's work.

bell loved reading and poetry as a child and began to write her own poems by the age of ten. She read everything she could get her hands on, from *Paradise Lost* to romance novels. When storms cut the power, her family would hold talent shows, and bell would recite her poems. She loved William Wordsworth and Emily Dickinson. Her love of books set her apart, and she was often disciplined for wanting to read instead of doing her chores, and for talking back to her parents.

After completing high school, bell received a scholarship to study at Stanford University in California, where she majored in English. The issues of race, gender, and class she had grappled with as a child were also present in her new surroundings. When she began to take women's studies courses, she quickly noticed the complete exclusion of Black women from the curriculum. No Black writers were included—no Black thinkers were discussed. She began writing her first major work, *Ain't I A Woman: Black Woman and Feminism*, while she was still an undergraduate, at the urging of her partner at the time, who responded to her frustration by encouraging her to write her own story.

bell graduated from Stanford in 1973 and enrolled at the University of Wisconsin for a Master's degree in English. Next, she moved to the University of California, Santa Cruz for a PhD in English. She published *Ain't I A Woman* in 1981 after extensive revision, and two years later completed her dissertation on the works of the writer Toni Morrison.

Ain't I A Woman was a controversial work that established bell as a major critical voice. She argued that the feminist movement failed to address the needs of poor and non-white women, as she had seen during her undergraduate education. Although it was criticized at the time for a lack of adherence to accepted academic norms—bell used no footnotes and provided no bibliography—the book has since become established as a major contribution to the field and is frequently assigned in college courses.

While continuing to write, bell also dedicated herself to teaching. She's described education as "the practice of freedom" and views teaching as a form of political resistance. After completing her dissertation, she continued to teach and published another book, *Feminist Theory: From Margin to Center*.

In 1985, she accepted a position in African American Studies at Yale University in Connecticut. The interdisciplinary nature of the department was important to her: she wanted to teach in a program where scholarship focusing on Black people would be seen as valuable and necessary.

A few years later, she moved to Oberlin College in Ohio, where she joined the Women's Studies faculty. Throughout the 1990s, bell continued to write and publish at an incredible pace. She published more than ten books in that decade, along with a number of journal articles. She moved to City College of New York in the mid-1990s, and finally to Berea College in Kentucky in 2004 to join the department of Appalachian Studies.

Now in her 60s, bell continues to teach, write, and lecture. Her substantial body of writing has profoundly influenced the field of feminist critique, and her work as a teacher has likewise impacted writers like Min Jin Lee, who as an undergraduate took a course with bell and described her presence in the classroom as "intense and crackling." Any girl who's interested in the life of the mind can take inspiration from bell's passion for writing and her tireless dedication to teaching and activism.

CHING SHIH

Arguably the most successful pirate of all time, Ching Shih ran an organization of approximately 70,000 pirates aboard some 1,200 ships and wielded considerable power along the South China coast during the early 19th century. (To give a sense of scale, the notorious pirate Blackbeard had four ships and 300 men.) While we don't know much about her as a person, historical records provide a thorough accounting of her pirate activities and the canny way she directed her fleet. One of the best sources of information about her is a book by an East India Company employee named Richard Glasspoole,

CHINESE JUNK SHIP

EUROPEAN GALLEON SHIP

who was held captive by Ching Shih's fleet and later wrote a first-hand account of his experiences.

Ching Shih means "Widow of Ching." She is also referred to as Cheng I Sao, or "Wife of Ching." (Ching, Cheng, and Zheng are different ways of writing the same Chinese name in Roman letters.)

Little is known about her early life. She was born around 1775 in Guangdong Province, on the southern coast of China bordering the South China Sea. This is all we know about her until 1801, when she married the pirate Cheng I. Legend has it that she accepted Cheng's proposal only after he promised her a share in his fleet, but there's no proof this actually happened. All we know for sure is that they did marry.

At the time of their marriage, piracy was flourishing in the South China Sea due to the sponsorship of the kingdom of Vietnam. A rebellion in Vietnam had depleted the kingdom's troops, and the king recruited Chinese pirates to serve him as privateers. But just a year or two after Ching Shih married her pirate husband, the rebellion was over, and with it, Chinese piracy in Vietnam. In the aftermath, Cheng I solidified his power and became the preeminent pirate along the South China coast.

In 1807, Cheng I died. Far from retiring to a placid widowhood, Ching Shih immediately made a bid for power and took control of the fleet. She secured the support of her husband's surviving kinsmen, convinced the squadron leaders of the fleet to transfer their allegiances to her, and, most importantly, selected a new leader to replace Cheng I: her husband's protégé and adopted son, Chang Pao. He would be completely loyal to her while also capably running the squadron and earning the respect of the other leaders of the fleet. (She later married him, ensuring his loyalty for good.)

With her power secure, Ching Shih set about formalizing the structure and day-to-day operations of the fleet. She extracted protection money from salt merchants, the villagers of the Pearl River Delta, and even the local navy! She also established a strict code of laws enforced by severe punishments: A pirate who deserted would have his ears cut off, and if a pirate took a wife from among the fleet's captives, he was expected to be faithful to her or risk execution. According to the captive Richard Glasspoole, these punishments were carried out with swiftness and vigor.

By 1809, the fleet's power along the coast forced the Chinese government to (reluctantly) seek help from the British and Portuguese, but tensions were also mounting within the fleet.

After several months of negotiations and the government agreeing to the pirates' conditions of zero punishment, the pirates came around to the idea of surrendering. The common sailors joined the army, and the leaders were offered military commissions and positions in the bureaucracy.

Now retired from her life of piracy, Ching Shih settled into her new existence as the wife of a military officer, Chang Pao, who was swiftly promoted to colonel and had two battalions under his command. After his death in 1822, Ching Shih returned to Guangzhou and settled there to raise her son and (possibly) run a casino. She died in 1844 at the age of sixty-nine, a wealthy woman with a respected role in society.

While many details about Ching Shih's life have been lost to history, what we do know makes it clear that she was a savvy leader with an impressive and successful career. The size and power of her fleet puts to shame the famous Caribbean pirates of the Golden Age of piracy. It's pretty cool that the world's most successful pirate was a woman!

SARAH McBRIDE

Sarah McBride made history when she publicly came out as transgender on the last day of her tenure as student body president at American University. Since then, she's made a name for herself in politics and LGBTQ activism. Not even thirty years old, she helped to pass anti-discrimination legislation in her home state of Delaware, spoke at the Democratic National Convention, and announced her candidacy for the Delaware Senate. Her courageous life and passionate activism can serve as a model for all Lumberjanes!

She was born in Wilmington, Delaware, in 1990, the youngest of three children. She knew from early childhood that she was a girl. In kindergarten, when boys and girls lined up separately, she longed to be in the girls' line. She described feeling like she was playing a game of dress-up: everyone else saw her as a boy, and she was forced to play along.

Sarah developed an interest in politics at an early age, and at thirteen started campaigning for a man who was running for state insurance commissioner. Through this work, she met a politician named Jack Markell who quickly took her under his wing. When he ran for governor in 2008, Sarah had her first paid job in politics as a field organizer for his campaign. On primary night, Sarah gave Jack's introduction speech. He won, and the taste of victory solidified Sarah's passion for politics. As governor, Jack continued to mentor Sarah, even requesting her assistance in writing speeches.

By this time, Sarah privately identified as transgender. The internet had shown her that she wasn't alone and that many other people had the same thoughts and feelings she did. She kept her gender a secret, though. With her political ambitions, she felt that she needed to hide the truth about who she truly was. If she told anyone, she feared that none of her dreams would come true.

Sarah began college at American University in Washington DC in 2009, and during her sophomore year decided to run for student body president. She won by a considerable margin and set about enacting LGBTQ-friendly initiatives

on campus. At the same time, her private struggles with her identity became so overwhelming that she thought about her gender "every single minute." She slowly began to come out, first to a friend from high school, then to her family, who were initially shocked and upset, but ultimately supportive. She came out to her mentor Jack Markell, who gave her his full support. Finally, she came out publicly with an article in her school's newspaper at the end of her junior year.

Sarah reveled in finally living openly as herself, something she described as "profound liberation." Her public coming out garnered enough attention that she was invited to a reception at the White House to celebrate Pride Month. There, she had a chance encounter with the man who would later become her husband: she literally bumped into him.

Her future husband, Andrew Cray, was a transgender lawyer and activist from Wisconsin who immediately became smitten with Sarah and contacted her online after the reception. They began talking, and a few months later went on their first date. Before long, they were inseparable.

That summer, Sarah began interning at the White House, the first openly transgender person to ever do so. She worked in the Office of Public Engagement, where she focused on issues of trans activism. She spent her fall semester there and learned the power of the personal touch in activism. For many of her colleagues, she was the first transgender person they had ever known, and conversations with Sarah were their first real exposure to trans issues.

Inspired by the experience, Sarah began volunteering with an organization in Delaware with the intent of passing non-discrimination legislation to protect transgender Delawareans. Delaware offered no protection from discrimination on the basis of gender identity. After a hard-fought battle and a last-minute amendment, the bill passed in the state Senate and House and was signed into law.

Sarah wasn't satisfied with victory for only Delawareans. She wanted all transgender people in the country to enjoy similar legal protections, and started a job with a progressive think tank in Washington to work on federal LGBTQ nondiscrimination protections. The focus of her team was the Employment Nondiscrimination Act, designed to protect sexual orientation and gender identity in the workplace. While Sarah felt this bill wasn't comprehensive enough—she wanted legislation that protected transgender people in all aspects of life, including housing and education—it was a starting point.

With her move to DC, Sarah also formally moved in with Andy. They were happy and deeply in love, and both thrived in their careers. But late that summer, Andy was diagnosed with cancer.

In the aftermath of his diagnosis, Andy proposed, and they were married on the rooftop of their building near the end of August, two years after they first began talking online. Andy died only a few days later, surrounded by friends and family.

Sarah's grief led to a deeper commitment to her political activism. Andy had dedicated his career to seeking healthcare protections for LGBTQ people, and Sarah wanted to honor his memory by continuing to fight for equality. She threw herself into her work, and began traveling around the country to give speeches for the Human Rights Campaign, a prominent LGBTQ lobbying group. She focused her efforts on a potential comprehensive LGBTQ civil rights bill that would provide protections not only in the workplace but also in housing, schools, hospitals, and public spaces. She and her colleagues produced a lengthy report, "We the People: Why Congress and US States Must Pass Comprehensive LGBT Nondiscrimination Protection." Sarah was the lead author.

In the spring of 2016, Sarah took the national stage when a selfie she took in a bathroom in North Carolina went viral online. The state had recently passed a controversial anti-transgender bill that limited access to bathrooms in public buildings to the gender marked on a person's birth certificate.

Not long after, Sarah left her work with the think tank and began working as the national press secretary for the Human Rights Campaign. She spent much of her time on the road, traveling and speaking to various groups. That summer, to her surprise and excited terror, Sarah was asked to speak at the Democratic National Convention in Philadelphia ahead of Hillary Clinton's acceptance of the nomination for president.

She was to be the first openly transgender person to speak at a major party convention. It was a pivotal moment for her, and also for the many transgender people who watched her speech. She described seeing, in the days following, pictures of transgender children watching her speech on TV, and knowing then that she had made history.

Sarah continues to work in politics and advocate for LGBTQ rights. In summer 2019, she announced her intention to run for the Delaware Senate, replacing a retiring Democrat. With her tireless commitment to equality and improving conditions for marginalized people, her awareness of her own privilege and her determination to help those less privileged, Sarah will certainly continue to do noteworthy things in the future. She's well worth keeping an eye on.

MARY ANNING

If you've ever been to a natural history museum, you might have seen the skeleton of a plesiosaur, an extinct marine reptile from the Jurassic Period. Twice the length of a human, their paddle-like flippers and long, slender necks make them distinctive. If you visit the Natural History Museum in London, you can see the first complete *Plesiosaurus* specimen ever discovered, a famous fossil uncovered by a woman named Mary Anning.

A great fossil hunter and early paleontologist, Mary Anning was born in 1799 in the town of Lyme Regis, England. Situated along the coast of the English Channel, Lyme Regis boasts ancient shale and clay cliffs that bear the fossils Mary spent her life searching out. In fact, the entire surrounding coastline, a span of nearly 100 miles, has yielded such a wide range of Mesozoic fossils that the region is now a designated World Heritage Site called the Jurassic Coast. (The Mesozoic is the geologic era from 252 to 66 million years ago, known as the Age of Reptiles. Dinosaurs lived during this time period.)

Mary was born to a poor family. Her father, Richard, was a cabinetmaker and carpenter, but he also collected and sold fossils as a side business. At the time, many local "fossilists" collected specimens and sold them to tourists as souvenirs. Interest in paleontology as a scientific discipline was growing, but to most people, these fossils were only curiosities. Mary and her brother Joseph first began fossil hunting as her father's apprentices, climbing around the cliffs near Lyme Regis to see what had eroded out during a winter storm or crumbled down a cliff face.

Richard tragically died in 1810 when Mary was only 11, leaving the family in debt and without any source of income. Mary and Joseph continued fossil hunting even after their father's death. The year after, Joseph found a skull of *Icthyosaurus*, an extinct marine reptile that looks something like a modern dolphin or porpoise. Mary found the rest of the skeleton a year later. This wasn't the first *Icthyosaurus* specimen to be found, but it was the most complete, and was met with much interest in London after it was sold to

MANY FOSSILS HAVE BEEN FOUND ALONG THE JURASSIC COAST,
LIKE LOBSTERS, AMMONITES, ECHINODERMS, AND
COPROLITES (AKA FOSSILIZED POOP!).

a collector. At this time, most people believed the history
of the world had been laid out in the Bible and that the
earth was only a few thousand years old. Fossil discoveries
challenged this belief and generated interest and excitement
from scientists who were beginning to think that the planet
was much older than previously thought.

Despite this success, the Annings continued to struggle
financially for the next decade or more. Joseph went to work

as an apprentice to an upholsterer and continued to help Mary search for fossils in his free time, although Mary was the family's primary fossil hunter. Complete skeletons of large vertebrates, which brought in the most money, were rare and could be difficult to sell, as evidenced by an 1821 letter from Mary's mother (also named Mary) to the British Museum pleading for payment for a fossil specimen the Annings had recently sold.

By 1823, Mary had gained some notoriety as an expert fossil hunter and began to have more financial success. She sold a small, well-preserved *Icthyosaurus* specimen for a good sum, and in December of that year made perhaps her most significant discovery: a strange, long-necked, small-headed creature. When the specimen was described to a meeting of the Geological Society early the next year, one of the members in attendance recognized it as a *Plesiosaurus*, which had previously been known only from fragments.

The specimen Mary had found was complete and remarkably well preserved. She was able to sell this specimen for about £100 (roughly £10,000 in 2020 money, or about $12,000).

With these successes, Mary became something of a local celebrity, and visitors traveled to Lyme Regis to meet her. Two 1824 accounts from visitors indicate that Mary was more than simply an intrepid fossil hunter: she was familiar with the anatomy of the specimens she found, read the scientific literature, and held strong opinions about the science of paleontology. She was also courageous, as fossil hunting could be dangerous work, involving long treks beneath hanging, crumbling cliffs. (In 1833, she barely escaped a landslide that killed her dog, Tray, who always accompanied her when she went collecting.)

1828 was another banner year for Mary. She was involved in work on coprolites (fossilized poop), playing an instrumental role by finding specimens that contained coprolites preserved within them, thus proving what these odd fossils were.

She also made another major fossil find, a *Pterodactylus*, one of the flying reptiles. This specimen represented the first British discovery of its type. Early the next year, she found another complete *Plesiosaurus*, and in December discovered *Squaloraja*, a fossil fish that represented an important transition between sharks and rays. Finally, in 1830, she made her last major discovery, a new species of *Plesiosaurus*.

She continued to hunt for fossils and sell them from her shop in Lyme Regis for the rest of her life, and in fact we don't know how many specimens present in museums today were Mary's discoveries. In 1838, in acknowledgment of her remarkable contributions to the geological community, the

British Association for the Advancement of Science awarded her an annual sum of £25 (about $3,000 in 2020 money). Her mother died in 1842, and Mary died a few years later, in 1847, after suffering from breast cancer for several years.

After her death, she received a number of tributes from the scientific community, including an obituary published in the quarterly transactions of the Geological Society, an organization that wouldn't even admit women until 1904, nearly 60 years later.

Despite Mary's incredible contributions to the field of paleontology, she went largely formally unacknowledged by the scientific community. While the collectors who purchased specimens from her were named and recognized in scientific papers, Mary as the discoverer was rarely given credit. Her working-class background, lack of formal education, and femaleness all conspired to limit her to a marginal role. Still, it's clear that she was highly regarded as a fossil hunter by the geologists and paleontologists of her time, and her remarkable career as a professional fossilist yielded invaluable information about evolution and the age of the Earth.

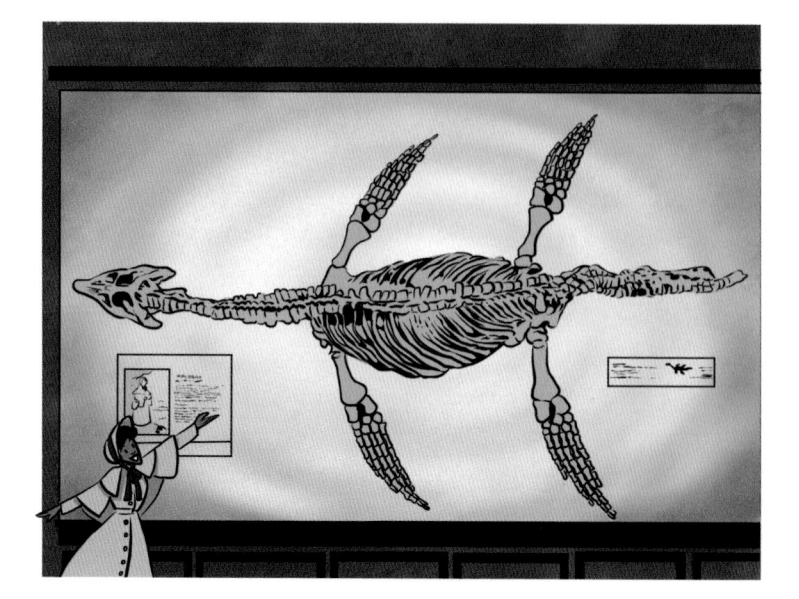

MARY'S PLESIOSAUR, FROM HER ORIGINAL SKETCH.

- Mary's sketch of her 1823 *Plesiosaurus* find shows each bone and its location in painstaking detail.

- *Plesiosaurus* was a predator species, feeding on fish and belemnites (extinct squid-like creatures).

SISTER ROSETTA THARPE

A pioneering gospel singer and early rock and roll musician, Sister Rosetta Tharpe wowed audiences with her stage presence and virtuoso guitar playing. Her 1945 hit single "Strange Things Happening Every Day" was a noted favorite of musicians like Jerry Lee Lewis and Elvis Presley and, along with other Black musicians of the time, influenced early rock and roll music. She has been inducted to both the Blues and the Rock and Roll Halls of Fame, securing her legacy as an important figure in the history of music.

Born in 1915 in Cotton Plant, Arkansas, Rosetta gained a reputation for her musical gifts early on in childhood. Both of her parents were musical: her father was a talented singer and played the guitar and harmonica, and her mother played the piano and mandolin. Rosetta's early musical education came from them and from their church, the Pentecostal denomination known as the Church of God in Christ. Gospel music was a crucial part of Pentecostal worship, and every Sunday Rosetta was exposed to the singing and instrumental accompaniment of services.

By the time Rosetta was six, her parents' marriage seems to have dissolved, and she and her mother moved to Chicago. There, she began performing in the church. She accompanied herself on guitar to great acclaim. Before long, she and her mother took their show on the road as traveling evangelists: Rosetta's mother, Katie, preached and Rosetta sang and played the guitar. On the circuit of tent meetings and revivals, Rosetta honed her techniques as a performer and mastered the art of showmanship. Even during the Depression, running and performing at revivals could be lucrative: Katie could make fifty dollars a week from running a revival, at a time when ten dollars a week was considered a good living.

By 1938, Rosetta had left her career on the gospel circuit and, accompanied by Katie, begun a secular career in New York City.

Not long after her arrival, Rosetta began performing at the famous Cotton Club on Broadway, which hosted all of the top musical stars of the day and was a favorite place to see and be seen. She was initially signed on a trial basis for a run of two weeks, one of many performers filling in between the main attractions. But her expressive, engaging performances made her a hit. Soon, she was offered a salary of $500 a week to perform at the Cotton Club. She signed with a talent agency, and not long after signed a contract with Decca Records, which under its "race" division also managed Louis Armstrong and Ella Fitzgerald. Rosetta's first recordings, from late 1938, sold so well that she was back in the studio by early 1939.

Rosetta's success at the Cotton Club was followed by gigs at the Paramount Theater, the Apollo Theater, and Carnegie Hall. Even so, she continued to perform at Pentecostal churches on Sunday mornings. Leaving the church for a secular career was a source of guilt for Rosetta, especially as church leaders disapproved of popular renditions of gospel songs. Rosetta expressed more than once that she loved and missed her church community. Still, she didn't leave New York and the income and acclaim she found there. She rubbed elbows with the likes of Duke Ellington and Cab Calloway, and she continued to perform and record. She soon began performing with Lucky Millinder's band and travelled all around the country with them. Even as World War II began, the band was as much in demand as ever.

Around the same time, Rosetta met Marie Knight, a young gospel singer, and the two began recording, performing, and

touring together. Life on the road wasn't always glamorous or easy, especially in the segregated South, where they couldn't even reliably find a place to spend the night. Still, Rosetta and Marie were successful and popular, until 1949, when tragedy struck and Marie lost her family to a house fire. In 1950, Rosetta and Marie split as a musical duo, although they remained friends for the rest of Rosetta's life.

Rosetta didn't skip a beat. She continued touring and recording with her backup singers, the Rosettes, and linked up with music promoters the Feld brothers in search of new ways to expand her audience.

The Felds pitched the idea of a combined concert and wedding—Rosetta only needed to produce a groom. Rosetta found him within a few months: a man named Russell Morrison, and in July 1951, roughly 20,000 people attended the concert/wedding at Griffith Stadium in Washington, DC.

Despite this success, Rosetta's career began to wane. The increasing popularity of the rhythm & blues format pulled interest from Rosetta's music. Her records flopped, and she played in smaller and smaller venues. But Rosetta refused to be defeated. She and Russell relocated to Philadelphia and made plans. Later that year, they embarked on her first European tour.

Europe was in the midst of a blues revival. Interest in the "authentic" music of Black Americans was at a peak, and Rosetta's tour was a resounding success. Audiences loved her, and she went on multiple tours of England and the

continent in 1957 and 1958, with such success that American news outlets began to report on her international renown. Buoyed by this positive press, she began to find a new welcome when she came home, as the American folk revival picked up steam. Rosetta was popular once more.

On tour in Europe in fall 1970, Rosetta had a minor stroke in Switzerland and was diagnosed with diabetes. After she returned home at the end of the tour, she resisted going to the doctor despite the urging of her friends. She ignored a diabetic ulcer on her foot for so long that her leg had to be amputated. Nonetheless, she kept performing until she died of a stroke in 1973.

In the past decade or so, renewed interest in Rosetta's work has led to public recognition and honors. A biography was published in 2007, and she was inducted to the Blues Hall of Fame that same year. In 2011, a four-hour documentary about her life aired on the BBC. An Off-Broadway play about her relationship with Marie Knight opened in 2016, and in 2018 she was at last inducted into the Rock and Roll Hall of Fame. It's safe to say she'll be remembered for her musical contributions for many years to come.

GRACE HOPPER

Considered a pioneer of computer programming, Grace Hopper was instrumental in developing COBOL, an early programming language. Within ten years of its invention, COBOL was the most widely used computer programming language in the world, and it's still in widespread use today. Grace's long and productive career began in the earliest days of modern computing, and she was a key figure in the early computer programming community.

Grace was born in New York City in 1906. She grew up on the Upper West Side as one of three children in the Murray family. Her father was an insurance executive and her mother was a mathematician, and Grace enjoyed an early life of privilege and education. She attended Vassar College, which at the time was a standard course for wealthy, educated young women. Less commonly, Grace went on to pursue graduate training at Yale University, where she received a doctorate in mathematics in 1934. After completing her degree, she began teaching at Vassar.

At Vassar, Grace gained a reputation as a popular and unorthodox teacher. She updated the curriculum for her courses and took an interdisciplinary approach that made mathematics relevant for students from many departments. Grace took advantage of a policy that allowed faculty members to audit courses for free and attended classes in architecture, geology, and philosophy, to name only a few.

She learned how to navigate Vassar's bureaucracy and to be an effective speaker and communicator, skills that would serve her well in the future.

After a decade at Vassar, Grace applied for a sabbatical to do research with a mathematician at New York University. During this fellowship year, Japan attacked Pearl Harbor, and the United States entered World War II the following day.

Grace, along with many of her friends and family, immediately sought to join the war effort. Instead of returning to Vassar, Grace took a position at Barnard College, where she taught a course intended to prepare mathematicians for the war. By now, she was tired of the long commute to Vassar and the predictable routine of teaching. She decided to join the Navy.

Although she was initially rejected for being too old and too underweight, Grace persisted, and in December 1943, two years after Pearl Harbor, she finally reported to the United States Naval Reserve Midshipmen's School in Massachusetts. Here, she was put through training designed to transform her from a civilian into an officer. Despite the rigors of military discipline and the intense coursework, Grace thrived, and she graduated first in her class.

Grace had anticipated being assigned to work as a codebreaker after graduation, but instead she was sent to Harvard to work on one of the world's first computers, officially called the Automatic Sequence Controlled Calculator, and informally called Mark I by the team at Harvard. Unlike modern computers, the Mark I was large enough to fill a room: it was eight feet high and more than fifty feet long. It could be programmed using paper tape encoded with step-by-step directions to perform a series of calculations, like a more sophisticated player piano. Invented by Lieutenant Commander Howard Aiken, who ran the project, the machine had originally been developed to ease the burden of hand-figuring the calculations for Aiken's doctoral dissertation. Now, it would serve the US as a secret weapon of war.

Grace received a chilly reception from Aiken, who was not pleased to have been sent a woman. Everyone else on the team was male. Immediately upon her arrival, she was assigned a daunting task: figure out how to use the Mark I in one week.

The unfamiliar machine came with no user manual. She was given a crude, slapped-together code book and told, in essence, to figure it out. After a crash course from one of the young ensigns on the team, Richard Bloch, a graduate student in physics who himself had only a few months of experience with the machine, Grace got to work.

First, she thoroughly acquainted herself with the machine's hardware, until she understood the purpose of every switch and relay. In this way, she came to understand the machine's limitations and how best to program it to perform calculations. The Mark I was very slow by today's standards—a simple multiplication took 10 seconds to compute. Grace decided it was better to manually program each calculation than to rely on the machine's automated functions, which were slower. Over the course of her first six months in the lab, Grace and Bloch developed an efficient system for programming the computer that lay the groundwork for future advances.

After the war was over, control of Mark I remained with the Navy, and Grace continued on at Harvard to work on the project. During the war, the Harvard team had been isolated from other groups working on early computers, but now that the pressure and secrecy of wartime had ended,

they began to communicate more with their colleagues at other institutions. Aiken had tasked Grace with writing an operating manual for the Mark I during the last year of the war, and she finished the manuscript for publication in late 1946. The first part of the manual consisted of a history of computing and the development of the Mark I. Along with three articles that were published in the journal *Electrical Engineering*, this manual summarized the accomplishments of the Mark I team.

The Navy's contract ended in 1949, and control of the project transferred to Harvard. Grace was on a three-year contract as a research fellow, and Harvard policy at the time prohibited the promotion of women. Her time was up.

Fortunately, by that time the burgeoning Association for Computing Machinery held regular meetings, and when Grace attended one, she was presented with multiple job offers. She eventually chose to join the private sector by accepting a position at the Eckert-Mauchly Computer Corporation in Philadelphia, a computer start-up working on building a vacuum-tube computer called the UNIVAC. In 1949, Eckert-Mauchly was sold to Remington Rand, an office equipment company, and much of Grace's time was devoted to traveling around teaching clients how to program.

Frustrated, in late 1951 she set about developing what came to be called a compiler. This compiler was Grace's attempt to teach computers to program themselves. Instead of manually providing instructions for every step of solving a mathematical problem, the user could input shorthand commands that the compiler would translate into very basic directions. The term "compiler" refers to the compilation of various subroutines into a cohesive program.

By 1954, Grace had convinced Remington Rand of the importance of her automated programming, and they created a new Automatic Programming Department. Grace wanted to develop a programming language based on familiar business vocabulary. This language, known as FLOW-MATIC, was made available to UNIVAC users starting in 1957. Grace was also heavily involved in the Association of Computing Machinery. Her efforts eventually led to the development of COBOL, an extremely successful programming language. While Grace is sometimes credited as the sole inventor of COBOL, this is not the case. Grace collaborated with programmers at the Department of Defense, IBM, the Radio Corporation of America, among others, to develop a common business language for programming. Through a series of meetings in 1959, they agreed on the basic nature of the language and set up committees. While several different programming languages were considered, FLOW-MATIC was eventually chosen as the primary model, with some input from other languages. The development of COBOL likely

WHILE GRACE DIDN'T ORIGINATE THE TERMS "BUG" OR "DEBUGGING" TO REFER TO COMPUTER ERRORS, SHE DID FIND A MOTH CAUGHT IN MARK I'S HARDWARE, LEADING HER TO NOTE, "FIRST ACTUAL CASE OF BUG BEING FOUND."

would not have been possible without Grace's organizational abilities and skill at collaboration and communication.

By the mid-1960s, Grace seemed to be preparing for retirement. She stepped down as Director of Automatic Programming Development and was placed on the retirement list of the Naval Reserve in 1966. Not long after, though, the Navy called her to active duty to help implement COBOL.

She was promoted to captain in 1973 and retired in 1986 as a rear admiral. She spent the last years of her life touring, lecturing, and working as a consultant, until she died in her sleep in 1992 at age 85.

Without question a skilled computer scientist, Grace also had an innate ability to collaborate with others, a combination which made her unstoppable. She thrived in the bustling community of computer programmers that sprang up after World War II. In her later years, she was much in demand as a speaker, and inspired many women interested in computer programming with her lively tales of the war years. Her three careers—college professor, computer programmer, and naval officer—show a powerful capacity for reinvention. Life is long, and Grace Hopper took full advantage!

ADA LOVELACE

Let's turn now from Grace Hopper to another, even earlier pioneer of computing: Ada Lovelace, the daughter of famous (some might say infamous) Romantic poet Lord Byron. Long before the first modern computer was invented, Ada saw the potential of a machine that could perform complex calculations beyond what a human could manage.

Ada was born Augusta Ada Byron in London in 1815. Her father, George Byron, was a poet and libertine. Her parents' marriage was brief and unhappy: they were married for barely a year before Ada's mother, Annabella, took her month-old daughter and returned to her parents' home, in a move that provoked much gossip and scandal.

Scarred by her experiences with the volatile, emotional Lord Byron, Annabella was determined that her daughter would grow up calm and rational. Ada was educated by tutors with a focus on mathematics, science, and languages.

Annabella was strict and distant and spent much of her time traveling around England seeking cures for her various physical ailments. Ada was raised largely by nannies and governesses, although she did spend more than a year traveling around Europe with her mother between the ages of ten and eleven. She was not a healthy child and was plagued by bad headaches. At the age of thirteen, she contracted a serious illness that left her legs paralyzed for a year and confined her to her bed for three. (This illness might have been measles or polio, but no one is really sure.) She wasn't able to walk without crutches until she was seventeen. During her long recovery, Ada used her time to read and study, and taught herself German.

Ada's new tutor, Mary Somerville, a self-taught scientist, quickly took Ada under her wing, even at times inviting Ada to stay with her family at their home. She encouraged Ada's intellectual interests and took Ada to scientific lectures.

The summer of her introduction to society at age seventeen, Ada met Charles Babbage, a 41-year-old mathematician and inventor, at a party at his home. Babbage gave a demonstration of a model of his Difference Engine, essentially an early calculator. Ada was entranced and she struck up a friendship with Babbage. She saw the mathematical possibilities of his invention and soon asked her tutors to give her more and more challenging instruction in mathematics. She wanted to use the Difference Engine to its full potential.

At age nineteen, Ada was introduced to the man who would become her husband: William King-Noel. (The name Lovelace comes from a title granted to William by Queen Victoria in 1838, making him Earl of Lovelace.) He was thirty and had been friends with Mary Somerville's son at Cambridge.

William was wealthy and titled and thus pleasing to Annabella, and seems to have pleased Ada enough that the two were married only a few months after their introduction, in June 1835. However, the marriage proved to be a disappointment to Ada—she and William had little in common, and she was frustrated by his lack of ambition. His main hobbies were agriculture and tinkering with their houses, and he showed little interest in Ada's studies, although he did support her pursuits.

Over the next four years, Ada gave birth to three children. As soon as they were old enough for schooling, Annabella took over their education, leaving Ada free to pursue her studies. She spent most of her time in London, where she was part of a social circle of intellectuals. In 1840, she began to work with a new tutor, a well-known mathematician named Augustus De Morgan, and devoted herself to her mathematical interests.

Babbage had continued to work on the Difference Engine and produced a new model that he called the Analytical Engine. This machine is sometimes considered the first computer. Similar to the Mark I that Grace Hopper worked with during World War II, the Analytical Engine was controlled by punch cards, an innovation taken from weaving looms.

Unfortunately, actually constructing the Engine wasn't possible with the existing technology for manufacturing machinery—modern computers and computer programming wouldn't develop for another hundred years! But Babbage convinced a young Italian scientist to write a paper on the machine, hoping that would increase the chances of government funding. The paper was published in French, and when Babbage needed an English translation, he turned to Ada.

Ada threw herself into the work. Her French was excellent, but a technical translation required great skill to accurately convey meaning to the reader. And Ada did more than simply

translate. She added notes to the end of the paper that clarified the Analytical Engine's operation and suggested how it might be used. She wrote that the machine could be used to play music or even games: things modern computers do, that no one else foresaw at the time. Perhaps most notably, she wrote out step-by-step directions by which the machine could calculate the Bernoulli numbers, an important sequence of rational numbers. The translation was published in 1843, when Ada was twenty-seven.

After her death in 1852, Ada's work with Babbage was largely forgotten for many years. In the 1930s, Alan Turing,

an extremely influential early computer scientist, conceived of a theoretical machine he called the Universal Computing Machine. He was familiar with Ada's work and quoted her in one of his papers. Around the same time, Howard Aiken, who invented the Mark I machine Grace Hopper worked with, was influenced by Babbage's Analytical Engine. While historians and computer scientists have argued over the value of Ada's contributions, there's no doubt she saw capabilities in Babbage's machine that no one else recognized.

KRYSTYNA CHOJNOWSKA-LISKIEWICZ

Imagine sailing around the world by yourself: just you, your boat, and the ocean and sky. If anything goes wrong, there's no one to help you. You're completely reliant on yourself, your ingenuity, and your skill as a sailor. That's the situation Krystyna Chojnowska-Liskiewicz faced as the first woman to sail alone around the world in 1976-1978. (The first man to sail solo around the world, Joshua Slocum, made his trip in the 1890s.)

Krystyna was born in Warsaw, Poland in 1936. She was raised in the small city of Ostróda in northern Poland, which is located near a number of lakes where Krystyna learned to sail. As a child, she encountered pictures of ships in a magazine and became entranced. When she was ready to enter university, she chose to study shipbuilding at Gdánsk University of Technology. There, she met her husband, Wacław.

After she graduated, Krystyna found a job as an engineer at the shipyards in Gdánsk. She received her captain's certificate in 1966 and began taking short ocean voyages.

In 1972, she and a crew of three other women sailed from Poland to Scotland, regarded at the time as either very reckless or very brave. A few years later, the Polish Yachting Association held a competition to select a woman sailor to make a solo trip around the world, and Krystyna won. Her husband designed her yacht, a thirty-two foot sloop called *Mazurek*.

Krystyna set out from the Canary Islands in March 1976, equipped with maps and a radio for weather forecasts. From there, she crossed the Atlantic Ocean to Barbados and sailed through the Panama Canal. She crossed the Pacific to Tahiti and then sailed on to Australia, where she spent some time in a hospital being treated for kidney stones. She sailed west across the Indian Ocean to Mauritius and then around the Cape of Good Hope at the southern tip of Africa. She finally returned to the Canaries (and her relieved husband) in April 1978, after a little more than two years.

Her trip wasn't without hazards and discomforts. At sea, she bathed in saltwater. She encountered frightening storms, and the fatigue of sailing a yacht alone was at times

overwhelming. But Krystyna persisted, and returned to Poland in triumph. Since her historic voyage, many other women have single-handedly circumnavigated the globe, but Krystyna was the first.

Krystyna sailed around the world on a 32-foot sloop called *Mazurek*, constructed of fiberglass laminated polyester. She circumnavigated the globe beginning and ending in the Canary Islands. Her route took her through the Panama Canal and around the Cape of Good Hope.

KRYSTYNA'S JOURNEY.

1976

March 28 - start to the cruise;
April 25 - call at Bridgetown, Barbados, stop until May 12;
June 4 - entry to Cristobal;
July 12 - passage of the Panama Canal and call at Balboa;
July 17 - from Balboa to the Pacific Ocean;
July 29 - crossing the Equator;
August 26 - call at Taiohae Bay at Nuku Hiva, stop until September 2;
September 10 - call at Papeete, Tahiti, stop until September 25;
October 25 - entry to Suva, Fiji, stop until November 7;
December 10 - entrance to Sydney.

1977

May 21 - departure from Sydney;
May 31 - call at Mooloolab, stop until June 7;
June 12 - da Mackay entrance, stop until June 18;
June 21 - entrance to Townsville, stop until June 23;
June 28 - call at Cairns, stop until July 2;

July 9 - entry to Cooktown, stop until July 14;

July 23 - arrival at Portland Road, from where the sailor was transported to the hospital due to kidney problems and returned to the yacht after a long recovery;

August 19 - exit from Portland Road;

August 21 - call at Thursday Island, stop until August 23;

September 2 - entry to Darwin, stop until September 17 and exit to the Indian Ocean;

November 15 - call at Port Louis, Mauritius, stop until November 22;

December 12 - a call at Durban.

1978

January 3 - leaving Durban;

January 21 - call at Capetown, stop until February 5, after leaving for a month no communication with the country;

March 20 - closing of the Earth loop;

April 21 - entrance to Las Palmas.

ANNE BANCROFT

Among the most acclaimed actresses of her generation, Anne Bancroft left her mark on Broadway and Hollywood. After getting her start in television, Anne had a forgettable early career in movies, then launched into fame with highly-praised theater roles. She worked steadily for five decades and earned acclaim throughout. She's one of only twenty-four people to win the so-called Triple Crown of Acting: an Academy Award, a Tony Award, and an Emmy Award.

She was born Anna Marie Italiano in New York City in 1931, the middle child of three daughters. Her father worked in the garment industry and her mother was a telephone operator. As a child, Anne loved to sing and perform, and she dreamed of being an actress. She joined the drama club in high school and began acting in school plays. Her drama teacher, impressed with Anne's abilities, encouraged her parents to send her to acting school. Despite the expense, they agreed, and Anne was accepted to the American Academy of Dramatic Arts in the fall of 1948 at the age of seventeen.

Anne graduated after two years and found some small roles in live television. At the time, the TV industry was based in New York, so she was able to live at home in the Bronx while she launched her career. In the fall of 1951, Anne got a call from her agent: Twentieth Century-Fox had seen a screen test she filmed the previous summer as a favor to a friend and wanted to offer her a contract.

Anne moved to Hollywood and began filming almost immediately. At the urging of the studio's head, who was worried about her being typecast due to her "ethnic" name, she picked her new stage name from a list. Her first role was a supporting part in a film starring Marilyn Monroe. She received positive reviews for her early films, and when her one-year contract was up, Fox renewed her for another year.

During her second year in Hollywood, Anne married a lawyer named Martin May. She later said she realized very quickly that the marriage was a mistake, and they separated after only two years of marriage. At the same time, her career in film hit a setback: Fox, faced with financial difficulties, didn't renew her contract a second time. But even as a freelance actress, she continued to find film roles. She made decent money, but the films tended to be low-budget and weren't well-received by critics. Frustrated, Anne felt that her career was going nowhere.

In early 1957, Anne decided to make a change. Newly divorced, she left Hollywood and moved back to New York, where she did some odd work in television to make ends meet.

That fall, she was cast in a Broadway play as the leading female role opposite the well-known actor Henry Fonda. *Two for the Seesaw* opened in January 1958 to glowing reviews.

Much of the praise focused on Anne's performance. In fact, she won a Tony Award for the role. Finally her acting had received the recognition she craved, but instead of resting on her laurels, she took voice and acting lessons and continued to work on her craft.

To prepare for her next role, as Annie Sullivan in *The Miracle Worker*, Anne studied sign language and worked with blind children. She won another Tony for the part, and the play was a huge success. When she left the play in early 1961, she immediately began preparing to film the movie version that summer. In the meantime, an appearance on Perry

Como's weekly television variety show led to an introduction to the comic and comedy writer Mel Brooks, who would become her second husband a few years later.

Anne's performance in the movie version of *The Miracle Worker* won her an Academy Award for Best Actress. Now established as a star, she continued to work in film and theater. Some of her ventures, like 1967's *The Graduate* (which proved to be the defining role of her career), were hugely successful, others were panned by critics. Anne was selective about the roles she took and at times only did a single project a year, reluctant to be away from Mel for too long as his career as a filmmaker and actor took off.

In 1972, at the age of forty, Anne gave birth to her only child, Max. She was thrilled to be a mother and took a year off work to spend with her new baby. She loved performing, though, and was soon back at work. The family relocated to Los Angeles, where they led a quiet domestic life of dinners with friends and picnics in the park while both Mel and Anne continued to pursue their careers.

Anne developed an interest in scriptwriting and directing, and in 1975 took a class in directing at the American Film Institute. Her feature-length debut as a director, *Fatso*, was released in 1980 to poor reviews and did not perform well at the box office. Anne didn't enjoy the experience of directing and never did it again.

Around this time, Anne was diagnosed with breast cancer, although she kept her illness private. Her cancer recurred repeatedly over the next few decades, even as she continued to work. Interesting roles for older women were in short supply, but Anne persevered and continued to seek out interesting scripts. In early 2004, Anne announced to some friends that she was having surgery for a tumor. Although the surgery was a success, Anne was later diagnosed with uterine cancer and underwent chemotherapy. Max and his wife had a son, Anne's only grandchild, whom she lived long enough to hold. She died in June 2005.

JANE GOODALL

Out of all living animals, chimpanzees are the most closely related to humans. But until the 1960s, we knew almost nothing about their behavior in the wild. Then Dame Jane Goodall, a young primatologist, established a field site in what is now Tanzania. In the decades of research that followed, Jane and her colleagues made many new and surprising discoveries about chimpanzee behavior and social life, which provided insight into our own early history.

She was born Valerie Jane Morris-Goodall in London in 1934. Her father, Mortimer, was a racecar driver, and her mother, Vanne, took care of the home and raised Jane and her younger sister, Judith. Jane's interest in animals and the natural world started early. In 1935, a baby chimpanzee named Jubilee was born at the London Zoo, and for her first birthday, Jane received a stuffed toy version of the little chimp. This quickly became her favorite toy. She loved *Dr. Doolittle* and *Tarzan* and dreamed of adventures in Africa.

After finishing school in 1952, Jane enrolled at Queen's Secretarial College to learn typing and shorthand. In 1954, with her training completed, she moved to Oxford to begin working and later accepted a different job in London. She was restless, though, and in early 1957 she accepted a school friend's invitation to visit her family farm outside Nairobi, Kenya. She fell in love with Kenya and found a job as a secretary in Nairobi, but her desire to work with animals remained strong. She got in touch with the prominent paleoanthropologist Dr. Louis Leakey, who had made important discoveries about early human evolution. On a tour of the museum, Jane and Louis hit it off, and he hired her as a secretary and took her to his field site at Olduvai Gorge for three months. Impressed with Jane's interest in the natural world, Louis began to make arrangements to have Jane study chimpanzees in the wild.

In summer 1960, with funding and permits secured, Jane and Vanne traveled to the Gombe Stream Game Reserve near Lake Tanganyika, which forms the western border of Tanzania. (The government insisted Jane have a chaperone, and her mother volunteered.) They settled into their camp, and Jane began the process of habituating the wild chimpanzees to her presence. For months, they ran away whenever they saw her. Over time, they became less frightened, and Jane learned to identify individual chimps and gave them names. One of the chimps, David Greybeard, soon provided two major revelations: that chimpanzees ate meat and used tools. Jane saw David eating a bush piglet, contradicting beliefs that chimpanzees were vegetarian.

DAVID GREYBEARD

FIFI

FRODO

GOLIATH

FLINT

PASSION

A few weeks later, she saw him using a long piece of grass to fish termites from their mound. At that time, scientists thought only humans were capable of making and using tools. When Jane sent word of her discovery to Louis, he famously responded: "Now we must redefine 'tool,' redefine 'man,' or accept chimpanzees as humans."

As Jane continued her field research, Louis made arrangements for her to earn a PhD at the University of Cambridge. This took some convincing, as Jane lacked an undergraduate degree. However, Louis prevailed, and in 1962 Jane enrolled at the university to begin her graduate studies, even as she continued her work at Gombe. She met her first husband, the wildlife photographer Baron Hugo van Lawick, when he came to Gombe to take pictures for the National Geographic Society. They married in 1964.

By the time Jane completed her PhD in 1965, she had developed an international reputation as a scientist and gained public recognition thanks to National Geographic articles and a documentary. A permanent research center had been constructed at Gombe to house the growing population of researchers and field assistants. Jane's only child, Hugo, (known as "Grub") was born in 1967 and spent his early years

at Gombe. She and Hugo van Lawick divorced in 1974, and Jane later married Derek Bryceson.

Over time, Jane became less involved in the day-to-day activities at Gombe as she devoted more time to conservation efforts. She founded the Jane Goodall Institute in 1977 to support research at Gombe; the organization has since expanded its efforts to conservation, community health projects, and sustainable agriculture. Today, Gombe is still a thriving research site, but Jane spends much of her time traveling and lecturing. She's internationally known both as an expert on chimpanzee behavior and as a committed conservation and animal welfare activist.

Jane's tireless field research provided invaluable insights into the behavior of wild chimpanzees. From her work at Gombe, we learned that chimpanzees have individual personalities, just like humans do. They fight; they play with their children; they have friends and enemies. In more recent years, Jane's conservation work has brought awareness to the threats of habitat loss and poaching this endangered species faces. If we're lucky, her work will mean there will still be chimpanzees in shaded forests for many generations to come.

HOW TO TERMITE FISH.

- Chimps begin termite fishing by finding a promising termite mound.

- Next, they select their tool: a stiff blade of grass, the stem of a plant, or a long stick.

- Sometimes they strip leaves from their selected tool or chew on the end to make it into a brush.

- Then, they dip their "fishing pole" into the termite mound. The angry termites bite the invader, and the chimp withdraws the stick or stem and enjoys a nice snack.

SYBIL LUDINGTON

"The British are coming!" This was the fabled cry of Paul Revere to warn fellow American patriots that British troops were approaching. (He didn't actually say it—his ride depended on secrecy and stealth.) His famous ride was immortalized by Henry Wadsworth Longfellow's poem, "Paul Revere's Ride." But he wasn't the only rider to make a midnight journey on horseback to rouse the countryside during the Revolutionary War. Two years after his ride, sixteen-year-old Sybil Ludington performed a similar feat of heroism in upstate New York.

Sybil was born in 1761 in Branford, Connecticut, the oldest of twelve children. Shortly after her birth, her parents moved to a farm in what's now Putnam County, New York, east of the Hudson River. The farm was prosperous, but Sybil grew up in a time of political unrest. Her father, Henry, was a prominent member of the community, active in local politics and the military. He was appointed colonel in the revolutionary militia in 1776. As the eldest daughter, Sybil helped keep watch for Loyalist forces who wanted to arrest her father.

Sybil's ride took place in the spring of 1777. British troops marched on Danbury, Connecticut, just over the border from New York, and burned houses and other buildings. A rider was sent to notify the Ludington household. Because it was planting season, Henry's regiment had been temporarily disbanded to tend to their farms, and they would have to be gathered to mount a defense of Danbury. With no one else available, he turned to Sybil.

She took a horse and rode through the night, from farm to farm, through heavily wooded land infested with brigands. It's thought she travelled some fifty miles to wake members of the regiment and tell them to spread the word: they would muster at the Ludington house at dawn. Henry's regiment and troops from Connecticut met with the British forces in Ridgefield, outside Danbury, and soundly defeated them.

Not much is known of Sybil's life after her ride. In 1784, she married Edmond Ogden, a former militiaman from Connecticut. They had one child, Henry.

In 1792, they moved to the town of Catskill on the Hudson River where Edmond worked as an innkeeper until his death in 1799 from yellow fever. Sybil purchased property in Catskill in 1804 and seems to have run her own tavern there. Her son trained as an attorney, and after the birth of her first grandchild, in 1811, Sybil moved with her son's family to Unadilla in central New York. She lived there for the rest of her life, helping to raise her six grandchildren. She died in 1839.

While Sybil's ride isn't as famous as Paul Revere's, she hasn't been forgotten. A statue of Sybil on a horse stands in Carmel, New York, and in the 1930s, Sybil's route and the location of the Ludington home were marked with signs. In 1975, she was commemorated with a postage stamp. Her heroic nighttime ride, performed at risk to her own life, shows that women weren't merely passive bystanders in the Revolutionary War. We remember Sybil's story, but there may be others we've forgotten.

BIBLIOGRAPHY AND FURTHER READING

1. Beyer, Kurt W. *Grace Hopper and the Invention of the Information Age*. Smithsonian Institution, 2009.

2. Cordery, Stacy A. *Juliette Gordon Low: The Remarkable Founder of the Girl Scout*s. Viking, 2012.

3. Daniel, Douglass K. *Anne Bancroft: A Life*. University of Kentucky Press, 2017.

4. Dacquino, Vincent T. *Patriot Hero of the Hudson Valley: The Life and Ride of Sybil Ludington*. The History Press, 2019.

5. Essinger, James. *Ada's Algorithm: How Lord Byron's Daughter Ada Lovelace Launched the Digital Age*. Melville House, 2014.

6. Francis, Conseula, ed. *Conversations with Octavia Butler*. University of Mississippi Press, 2010.

7. hooks, bell. *Bone Black: Memories of Girlhood*. Henry Holt and Company, 1996.

8. hooks, bell. *Wounds of Passion: A Writing Life*. Henry Holt and Company, 1997.

9. McBride, Sarah. *Tomorrow Will Be Different: Love, Loss, and the Fight for Trans Equality*. Crown Archetype, 2018.

10.   Murray, Dian. *"One Woman's Rise to Power: Cheng I's Wife and the Pirates." Historical Reflections*, vol. 8, no. 3, 1981, pp. 147-161.

11.   Peterson, Dale. *Jane Goodall: The Woman Who Redefined Man.* Houghton Mifflin, 2006.

12.   Schultz, Glady Denny, and Daisy Gordon Lawrence. *Lady from Savannah: The Life of Juliette Low.* JB Lippincott, 1958.

13.   Testa, Jessica. "The Strongest Woman in America Lives in Poverty." *Buzzfeed*, https://www.buzzfeed.com/jtes/the-strongest-woman-in-america-lives-in-poverty.

14.   Torrens, Hugh. *"Mary Anning (1799-1847) of Lyme; 'the greatest fossilist the world ever knew.'"* British Journal for the History of Science, vol. 28, 1995, pp. 257-284.

15.   Turnbull, Stephen. *Samurai Women 1184-1877.* Osprey Publishing, 2010.

16.   Wald, Gayle F. *Shout, Sister, Shout! The Untold Story of Rock-and-Roll Trailblazer Sister Rosetta Tharpe.* Beacon Press, 2007.

17.   Wright, Diana E. *"Female Combatants and Japan's Meiji Restoration: the case of Aizu."* War in History, vol. 8, no. 4, 2001, pp. 396-417.

DISCOVER
ALL THE HITS

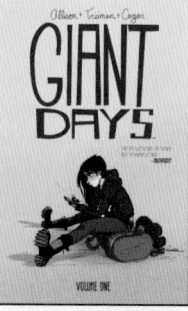